LIFE CYCLE OF A
CHICKEN

by Noah Leatherland

Minneapolis, Minnesota

Credits

All images are courtesy of Shutterstock.com. With thanks to GettyImages, ThinkstockPhoto, and iStockphoto. Cover – Vector_Up, irin-k, Eric Isslee. Recurring images – gravity_point, yugoro, The_Pixel, Iyeyee, Voin_Sveta, nataliiudina, ozzichka, johnjohnson. 2–3 – Sorbis. 4–5 – Eric Isselee, VP Photo Studio. 6–7 – Ethan Daniels, Laura Dts. 8–9 – Francisco Blanco, Svetlana Foote. 10–11 – aaltair, frank60, photowind. 12–13 – Emőke Dénes (Wikimedia Commons), Jose Barquero. J, Paul Starosta. 14–15 – Jesus Cobaleda, Nick Pecker. 16–17 – Yuliko Agnieszka Bacal, Debbie Steinhausser, Anna Violet. 18–19 – Agami Photo Agency, John Navajo, Vishnevskiy Vasily. 20–21 – Chanasid kaewpirun, Novim images. 22–23 – Keri Delaney, Rob Hainer.

Library of Congress Cataloging-in-Publication Data

Names: Leatherland, Noah, 1999- author.
Title: Life cycle of a chicken / by Noah Leatherland.
Description: Minneapolis, Minnesota : Bearport Publishing Company, [2025] | Series: Life cycles on the farm | Includes index.
Identifiers: LCCN 2023059633 (print) | LCCN 2023059634 (ebook) | ISBN 9798889169581 (hardcover) | ISBN 9798892324861 (paperback) | ISBN 9798892321228 (ebook)
Subjects: LCSH: Chickens--Juvenile literature. | Chickens--Life cycles--Juvenile literature.
Classification: LCC SF487.5 .L43 2025 (print) | LCC SF487.5 (ebook) | DDC 636.5--dc23/eng/20240129
LC record available at https://lccn.loc.gov/2023059633
LC ebook record available at https://lccn.loc.gov/2023059634

© 2025 BookLife Publishing
This edition is published by arrangement with BookLife Publishing.

North American adaptations © 2025 Bearport Publishing Company. All rights reserved. No part of this publication may be reproduced in whole or in part, stored in any retrieval system, or transmitted in any form or by any means, electronic, mechanical, photocopying, recording, or otherwise, without written permission from the publisher. Bearport Publishing is a division of Chrysalis Education Group.

For more information, write to Bearport Publishing, 5357 Penn Avenue South, Minneapolis, MN 55419.

Contents

What Is a Life Cycle?. 4
Chickens on the Farm 6
Laying Eggs 8
Inside the Egg 10
Time to Hatch. 12
Chirping Chicks 14
Juveniles 16
All Grown Up 18
The End of Life. 20
Life Cycle of a Chicken 22
Glossary 24
Index 24

WHAT IS A LIFE CYCLE?

All living things go through different stages of life. We come into the world and grow over time. Eventually, we die. This is the life cycle.

As humans, we start life as babies. We grow into toddlers and children. Then, we become teenagers. Finally, we are adults and get even older. We may have babies of our own, and then the cycle begins again.

CHICKENS ON THE FARM

Animals on the farm go through life cycles, too. Farm chickens are **domestic** birds. This means they are not wild. People keep them as **livestock**.

There are more than 60 different kinds of chickens.

Some farms have only a few chickens, while others have hundreds or thousands. Farmers raise these birds for their meat and to gather the eggs they lay.

LAYING EGGS

All chickens start out as eggs. **Female** chickens, called hens, build nests where they lay these eggs. A hen sits on her nest to keep the eggs warm.

A hen usually lays about one egg a day.

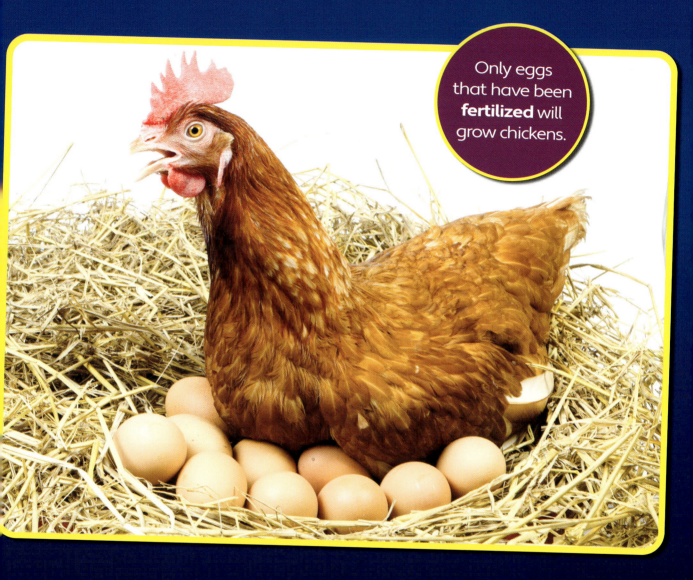

Only eggs that have been **fertilized** will grow chickens.

A group of eggs is called a clutch. The hen turns her eggs over a few times a day to keep the chicks inside healthy.

INSIDE THE EGG

A baby chicken starts off as a tiny **embryo** inside one of these eggs. It eats the egg yolk. The **nutrients** in this food help it grow. Over time, the chick fills the inside of the egg.

Chicks may start chirping inside their shells within about 19 days.

A liquid inside the shell, called the egg white, keeps the baby and yolk safe as the baby grows. So does the hard shell of the egg.

TIME TO HATCH

After about 21 days, the baby starts to **hatch**. The chick begins to work its way out of the shell.

EGG TOOTH

The chick uses a sharp point on its beak called an egg tooth to peck through the eggshell. It takes about 24 hours for the chick to make a hole large enough for it to get out.

CHIRPING CHICKS

A chick is wet when it hatches. It begins to dry once it is outside of the egg. Sometimes, farmers keep chicks in warming boxes to help them dry completely.

Pecking through the eggshell can be tiring. A chick may fall asleep soon after hatching.

Once dry, the chick has fluffy feathers called down. These help keep the chick warm. The baby

JUVENILES

Chicks eat lots of food, including grains and bugs. They grow into **juvenile** chickens, which is like being a teenager for humans. During this part of the life cycle, the chickens get larger and start growing their adult feathers.

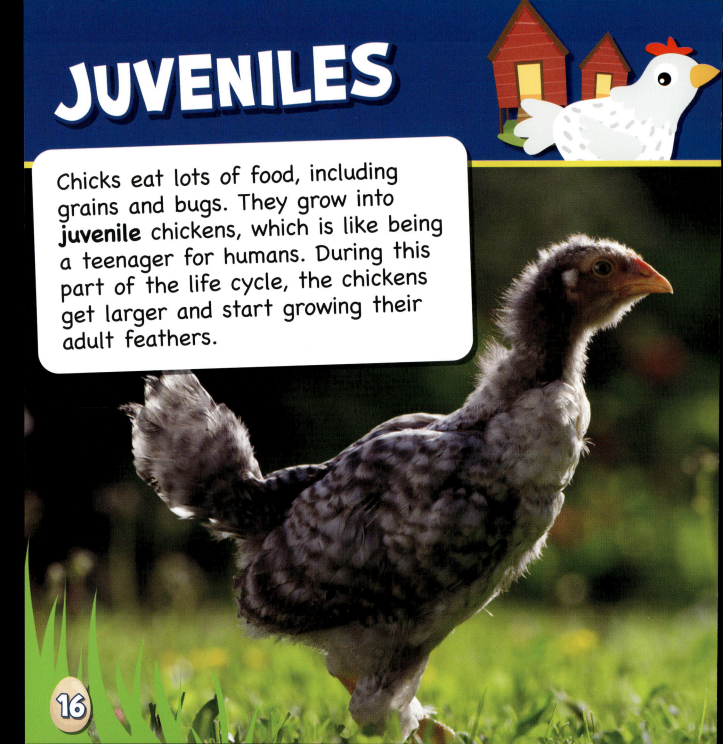

Mother hens stop looking after their chicks when they become juveniles.

Juvenile chickens look thinner and smaller than adults. In a group of chickens, the adults eat before the juveniles do. This is called the pecking order.

ALL GROWN UP

Chickens are adults by the time they are about one year old. These birds have all of their adult feathers.

Adult chickens can be about 30 inches (70 cm) tall.

A hen can lay as many as 300 eggs per year.

When they are fully grown, hens can lay their own eggs. Soon, their clutches will hatch into even more chicks.

THE END OF LIFE

Chickens have many **predators**. Foxes, raccoons, snakes, and cats may sneak onto farms and hunt chickens. Most farmers build fences and train other animals to keep their birds safe.

Dogs, geese, and donkeys are often used to keep chickens safe.

Chickens can live for about eight years. However, chicken raised for their meat usually don't live this long.

LIFE CYCLE OF A CHICKEN

A chicken begins its life as an egg and hatches into a chick. Then, it grows into a juvenile. Eventually, it becomes an adult.

During its life, a hen may lay eggs and have chicks of its own. Eventually, the hen will die, but the chicks live on and have even more chickens. This keeps the life cycle going!

Glossary

domestic tamed for use by humans

embryo an unborn or unhatched animal in the early stages of growth

female a chicken that can lay eggs

fertilized made able to grow into a baby animal

hatch to break out of an egg

juvenile young and not fully grown

livestock animals that are raised by people on farms or ranches

nutrients substances needed by plants and animals to grow and stay healthy

predators animals that hunt and eat other animals

Index

chicks 9-10, 12-16, 19, 22
eggs 7-11, 13-14, 19-20, 22-23
egg tooth 13
embryos 10-11
farms 6-7, 20-21
feathers 15-16, 18
hen 8-9, 15, 19, 23
juveniles 16-17, 22
nest 8
predators 21